One Room Out West

One Room Out West

The Story of the Jore Schoolhouse
and its Students

Rita Seedorf

EASTERN WASHINGTON UNIVERSITY PRESS

SPOKANE, WASHINGTON

We gratefully acknowledge the generous support of Eastern Washington University's College of Education and Human Development in making this book possible.

Library of Congress Cataloging-in-Publication Data

Seedorf, Rita.
 One room out west : the story of the Jore School and its students /Rita Seedorf.
    p. cm.
  ISBN 0-910055-84-X (pbk. : alk. paper)
  1. Jore School (Newport, Wash.)--History. 2. Jore School (Newport, Wash.)--Students. 3. Rural schools--Washington (State)--History. I.
Title.
LD7501.N73 S44 2002
372.9797'77--dc21

                              2002014573

Table of Contents

For Shirley Anne (Davis) Anderson, BAE '66
July 27, 1945—June 18, 2002
Who worked tirelessly for the preservation of the stories and artifacts
of the one-room schoolhouses.

Acknowledgments

I am grateful to the many people who helped with this project. At Eastern Washington University President Steve Jordan, Fritz Erickson, Dean of the College of Education and Human Development, and Jerry Logan, Chair of the Department of Education all provided encouragement and support for the project. Judy Rogers of the EWU Foundation put me in contact with former teachers and pupils of the Jore and other one-room schools and kept me on the project with constant and cheerful reminders. The members of the Cheney Normal School Heritage Steering Committee also provided me with support and suggestions of people to interview. Charles Muetschler, university archivist provided advise and materials from the early schools of Washington State. Susan Beemer of the Washington State Archives was a tremendous help in locating the records of Stevens County School District #46 and Pend Oreille School District #22 and digging them out from their storage place somewhere under a football field. The Pend Oreille County Historical Society, particularly Evelyn Reed, Faith McClenny, and Alice (Crysler) Warner who provided pictures, records and help in locating former Jore School pupils. I also need to thank former Jore School pupils Lucy Graham Van Ness, Katherine Burley Ritland, Ivan Troyer, Twylah Giem, and Ron Geaudreau and all the other teachers and pupils of one room schools who shared their stories with me. I also want to thank Joelean Copeland of Eastern Washington University Press who made the editor-author relationship a very positive experience. Finally, I owe a debt of gratitude to my family members who helped on many projects and listened to stories of the one-room schoolhouse for over two years.

The newly restored Jore Schoolhouse on the campus of Eastern Washington University in Cheney, Washington.

Introduction

The one room schoolhouse, independent and isolated, called students from the surrounding homestead shacks and farmhouses. They came by foot, horseback, wagon, and later car to spend six hours reading, writing, and ciphering,[1] with lunch and recess providing welcome breaks. Attendance was irregular, but students came as often as they could during the school year. When thought ready, they stood for the eighth grade exam proving they had mastered the curriculum. The history of the Jore one-room schoolhouse came to life through the memories of former students and members of the Jore family.

The one-room schoolhouse arrived on the campus of Eastern Washington University the morning of August 17, 2000. Students, faculty, staff, and interested bystanders waited patiently as the 20 by 40-foot building inched into place. For Dr. Charles Miller, Professor of Education at EWU, the presence of a one-room schoolhouse on campus fulfilled a dream he had been working on for over a decade. In fact, he had begun his teaching career in a two-room schoolhouse over 50 years earlier and felt a one-room schoolhouse on campus would stand as a testament to the university's origin. According to Miller, "The historic significance of the one-room schoolhouse in building a democracy is a legacy that I had hoped to pass on to future teachers. It symbolizes our heritage of providing education for all citizens."[2]

Charlie Miller travelled the Pacific Northwest countryside for years, searching for the perfect one-room schoolhouse. Some, he discovered, were privately owned, while others were completely ravaged by time and nature. In 1997, he located a sturdy one, but it burned to the ground before the University could acquire it. Miller was not easily discouraged, and he and his wife, Carolyn, resumed their Sunday drives in search of an appropriate building.

Finally during Christmas 1999, he found the Jore (pronounced Jury) schoolhouse in the woods near Newport, Washington. Officially called the Diamond Lake School, families in the area called it the Jore School in honor of the homesteader who donated land for the building site.

Time had been kind to the structure, which rested on a cement foundation and covered with a metal roof. Miller knew this was the right building, but the matter of gaining title and raising money for renovation stood between him and his dream.

Football tickets and a local credit union helped Miller's dream along. But most important, Eastern Washington University's President Steven Jordan became enthusiastic about the prospect of bringing a one-room schoolhouse to the Cheney campus (Jordan had recently come from Kansas where one-room schoolhouses were plentiful). When Jordan and Mike Irish, Eastern's Associate Vice President for Facilities, arrived to look at the school, Jordan stated, "We've got to get this. This is an essential part of the history of education in the Inland Northwest."[3]

Gaining title to the building was complicated because the land changed hands shortly after Miller located the building. The new owner, Riley Lumber Company, agreed to give the building to the university in exchange for four tickets to that season's EWU-University of Montana football game. The next challenge was financing the 50 mile move to EWU's campus.

The Spokane Teacher's Credit Union became

interested in the project after Judy Rogers of the Eastern
Washington University Foundation approached them
about fund raising opportunities. She mentioned the
schoolhouse project and they enthusiastically agreed
to make a substantial donation of $62,000.[4] The journey
began August 14, 2000, after professional movers
removed the bell tower and rolled wheels under the
school's foundation in preparation for the journey to
the Cheney campus at five-miles-an-hour through
secondary roads and was covered extensively by local
media during the two days and nights the school was
on the move.[5]

The Jore School's original location near Newport, Washington.

EWU President Steven Jordan, Dr. Charlie Miller, and Associate Vice President for Facilities Mike Irish before the school's journey to Cheney.

A great deal of preparation went into the Jore School before it could be transported to Eastern Washington University's campus. This included removing the building from the original foundation, removing what remained of the roof, and removing all inside plaster work.

The dedication plaque outside the Jore School, now The Cheney Normal School Heritage Center on the campus of Eastern Washington University.

Betsie and John Jore with daughters Sara and Lena, 1882.

Photos courtesy of Barbara Yonck

John and Betsie Jore ca. 1911.

Photos courtesy of Barbara Yonck

A History of the Jore Schoolhouse

The "Jore School" got its name from the family who donated the land for the building. John Olsen Jore, wife Betsie, and their children moved to Newport in 1890 and claimed a homestead of 160 acres.[6] Married in 1878, the couple had 14 children. However, only seven daughters and one son lived to adulthood. The graves of several Jore children remain on the hillside above the site occupied by the school.[7] Grandma Jore, as Betsie was known to early day school children, stood only four feet, eleven inches tall, smoked a corncob pipe, and always had her pockets stuffed with horeshound candy, a confection made from a bitter mint.

The Jore School (or Diamond Lake School District) was formed in 1891, and the first school building, a shed with vertical siding and few windows, was constructed in 1892. There is no record of what became of this building, though it is believed to have burned. The present building with its bell tower, double doors, and white washed siding was constructed in 1905 at the junction of Deer Valley Road and Coyote Trail. The school district began as Stevens County School District #46 and later became Pend Oreille School District #22

Photos courtesy of Barbara Yonck

Betsie Jore and her son-in-law, Gerald Adams Calhoun in 1936.

when Stevens County was divided in 1911 due to population growth.

The residents of Newport tried for several years to create a county of their own. There were no roads over the mountains at that time, making travel from Newport to the county seat at Colville a three or four day trip with a lay-over in Spokane. A petition asking the legislature to create Pend Oreille County was signed by

1500 citizens of the future county. The people of Stevens County voiced no objections, and in May 1911, Governor Hay signed the act passed by the legislature. The county was recognized on June 10, 1911, with the temporary county seat located in Newport.

The 20 by 40-foot school building had nine windows on the east side and two on the west. Four wooden steps led to a porch that spanned the front of the building,

Photo courtesy of Pend Oreille County Historical Society.

The original Jore School and the first class in 1892. The building is believed to have burned and was rebuilt in 1905.

and a bell tower with shutters rose above the cloakrooms beyond the two front doors. Near the road was the horse barn built sometime between 1918 and 1925.

The Jore School front doors were originally designed so boys and girls could enter separately and hang their coats in different cloakrooms lined with hooks and shelves for lunches. However, some former students don't remember the doors being used in that way. When Katherine Ritland attended the school between 1917 and 1925, she recalled the entry hall for coats was on the right side, and the left entry hall held a cupboard where students could leave their lunches or supplies.[8] Twylah Giem attended the school between 1925 and 1928 and remembered the right entryway was the place to hang coats and the left entryway a library.[9]

The stove was the heart of the school and generated a great deal of work. During the long winters, teachers arrived early to clean out the ashes and start a fire to warm the schoolroom. Its warmth would also keep some lunches from freezing while heating others to an edible temperature. In most schools, including the Jore School, the stove was kept hot all night by spreading ashes over the coals set in place the day before. When stoves got too hot, the students' crayons melted.

Students worked at desks that seated one or two

persons. The wooden desktops rested on ornate iron bases, slanted toward the occupant, and nailed to runners on the floor, usually with the shortest desks toward the front of the room and the bigger ones in back. An indentation near the top of the surface kept pencils from sliding off and a hole was drilled in the top right corner of the desk to hold an inkwell. Books slid into a shelf underneath the hinged desktop.

Blackboards lined the walls and were full of lessons. Blackboards near the recitation bench were always left blank so students could demonstrate their problem solving skills.

The school was surrounded by a playground, four-stall horse barn, woodshed, and double outhouse. The well and pump that supplied water for the school stood in the middle of the playground. A teacherage with a connected woodshed and outhouse stood to the right of the schoolhouse.

Winter entertainment was provided by a nearby hill. When snow fell, the children loved to rid their sleds or the teacher's skis. Because recess was unsupervised, there were bumps and bruises; during the 1926-1927 school year, a student was slightly injured when his sled hit the flagpole at the bottom of the hill.

The teacher's cottage, called a teacherage, was added

to the school grounds in 1923 or 1924.[10] The two-room cottage, built slightly behind the schoolhouse, included a kitchen with an indoor pump. Before its construction, teachers who could not get home each day boarded with the Jore family.

The first teacher to live in the teacherage was Mary B. Headrick, who before the cottage's completion, commuted two miles daily from her family's farm. In the winter, she occasionally had overnight guests, such as Katherine Ritland and her older sister who could not make their one-mile country walk in heavy snow. Parents had to trust the teacher's good judgment because, with no telephones, there was no way for anyone to inform them of students' whereabouts. Between 1926 and 1928, Madelyne Black lived full-time in the teacherage with her younger brother, Donald, who also attended the Jore School. The following year, another local child, Ron Geaudreau, lived there with his mother, Stella.

Having a well on the school's ground was a luxury. At some schools, water was hauled from a nearby creek, spring, or the nearest farmer's well. Generally, the larger, stronger boys were sent while the teacher watched through the classroom windows.

Former students remembered much about the school

and surrounding buildings, but the outhouses generated the most stories. The Jore School had a two-seated toilet—one side for the boys and one side for the girls. Ron Geaudreau remembered while he was a first grader at Colockum, a school near Wenatchee, Washington, two sheep hung around the school. "The ram, for some reason, would push me down all the time. One day, I raised my hand to go to the outdoor privy. When I got outside, there was that darned ram. The privy door was open and he ran in first. I closed the door and latched it and went behind the privy to complete my original mission and returned to the schoolroom. Sometime on the following Sunday someone was going past and heard a commotion. The door was opened and that ram ran toward the river."[11]

Toilet paper was often a luxury. Usually, parents were asked to cut their old Sears and Roebuck catalogs into squares and send them to school with their children. These squares were then hung on a nail inside the schoolhouse door, and as the children were excused to use the privy, they took as they many sheets as thought they would need.

Quite a few families lived at the Jore farm, about two or three blocks down the road from the school. Four

Photo courtesy of Pend Oreille County Historical Society.

Madelyne Black in front of the Jore School in 1927. She taught at the school during the 1926–1927 and 1927–1928 school years.

of the Jore children, Tillie, Annie, May, and Hannah, along with children from the Anderson, Rien, Tarbet, and Fowler families are pictured in front of the first school building, erected in 1892. Later the youngest child, Mabel Jore, appeared on the school census. Many of the Jore grandchildren also attended the school including Marion, Irene, Carrie, and Henry Vannier, Gladys and Helen Van Pappelendam, Earla and Ila Mongan, Elaine Johnson, and Virgil Jore.[12]

Many of the men connected to the Jore Family served as school board members, according to the school documents of the 1890s, beginning with John O. Jore. His brother-in-law, K.O. Felland, and three of John Jore's sons-in-law, George Vannier, Elmer Bishop, and John Van Pappelendam, were also school board members.[13]

The school continued in its original capacity for 24 years and closed in 1929 when consolidated with the Newport School District. Students then travelled seven miles to Newport to attend classes.

For the next 71 years, the school served as a house and a storage shed before moving to EWU's campus. It was abandoned when Dr. Miller found it; the doors had been removed and there was evidence that it had been used for partying by vandals.

The schoolhouse is now an integral part of the

Eastern Washington University campus. Its bell signals the new school year and rings at the beginning of Commencement each June. Visitors from an older generation are reminded of their past and younger generations get glimpses of a life without electricity, indoor plumbing, or automobiles; a life they can only imagine.

Jore School Families

The children of the Jore School came from families who worked the forested lands of Pend Oreille County for their livelihood, selling firewood and planed lumber to customers in Newport and Spokane. These families were severely affected by the forest fire that roared through the area in 1910, scarring the landscape and leaving many homeless. The remaining trees were cut into logs and sold to growing communities nearby. When the land could no longer support the families, fathers worked away from home, returning only on the weekends. Most families also augmented their income with gardens and kept chickens for meat and eggs. Life for the Jore School families was centered on these traditions and around occasional trips to the "big city" of Newport seven miles northeast.

Newport played an important role in the life of the school district. It was the market center where extra produce from family gardens was sold and where families bought supplies they could not raise on their own land. These excursions into town were great adventures for some of the children whose lives were normally bounded narrowly by farm and school. Once a student's education at Jore was complete, he or she attended Newport High School. This was sometimes a hardship on families, and parents lived apart to keep the children in school and put food on the table for those still at home. Mothers would rent homes or apartments in town and live with the children during the school year while husbands stayed on the farm. Less frequently, the children moved to town alone to board with families there.

Dressing warmly enough to get to school was challenging during the winter months. Girls were required to wear dresses, but in very cold weather, they were allowed to wear pants underneath. Of course, these had to be removed when they arrived at school. Girls' dresses and boys' shirts were usually made by their mothers and, since most of them were cut from old feed sacks, looked a lot alike. Children's shoes were chosen for durability and were protected from the rain, mud, and snow by overshoes, which were always removed inside the schoolroom. One small boy refused to remove his overshoes until his teacher, Ruth Foster, insisted. She was shocked to discover he was wearing neither shoes nor socks underneath, and his feet were frozen. She thawed out his feet, wrapped them in rags, put her own anklets on the child, and sent him home with a note that he wasn't to return wearing only overshoes.[14]

The cold was an enemy even to those children who were given rides to school. Bricks or rocks were heated in the stove, wrapped in cloths and put at the feet of the children who were bundled up in blankets. For evening events, such as the Christmas program, entire families arrived in wagons at the school and placed their bricks and stones near the school stove to warm them for the trip home.

* * * * * * * * * * * * * * * *

Five students who attended the Jore School between 1914 and 1929 retell memories about their life and education at the Jore School: Lucy Graham (Van Ness), Katherine Burley (Ritland), Ivan Troyer, Twylah Giem (Keplinger), and Ron Geaudreau as well as descendents the Smith Family whose four sons attended the Jore School.

Lucy Graham

Lucy Graham, attended the Jore School along with her older sisters Jenny, Kate and Maude. She started school in Fall 1914, when she turned six.[15] She had already visited the Jore School several times with her sisters before enrolling as a first grader. The girls would walk to school in the winter; their short legs and deep snow made the walks cold and long. Lucy sat in a small seat in the front of the room and when her teacher, Ella McDowell, called for the first graders, she and two other children, would to come up to the recitation bench.

At the recitation bench, students would be asked to preform a number of tasks including reading aloud from a selected passage to test their reading and vocabulary skills, responding to verbal quizzes, and solving mathematical problems on the blackboard. Once done, the teacher would tutor the student in problem areas and assign new lessons.

Lucy's father, Wilfred (Babe) Graham and his brothers, Charles and Alfred, ran sawmills in the area. The family moved each time the tree stands near their home became exhausted. Each time the mill moved, the family had to build a new house and a new bunkhouse for the hired men who worked at the mill. The houses were all built with the same plan: the dining room for the loggers in the front with a kitchen connected to the living room and three bedrooms at the rear of the house.

Lucy tagged along when her mother, Kate, went to Newport for groceries needed to cook the three meals a day for her family and the hired men. Dave, one of her father's teamsters, would drive them to the grocery store where Lucy's mother would drop off the weekly order to be filled. Next, mother and daughter would run errands around town and visit friends if time allowed. On these shopping days, Lucy remembered having a rare restaurant meal when the two ate their noontime dinner in town.

While the women were in town, Dave fed and watered the horses and then spent the rest of the day in the saloon. When it was time to pick up the groceries and return home, Lucy and her mother would walk to the saloon to get Dave. Since respectable women did not enter saloons, Kate always asked one of the men who were constantly hanging around the front of the building to get their driver. Lucy recalled that, after spending the day at the saloon, Dave was always exceptionally happy as he drove them all back to the mill.

While Lucy was a student at the Jore School, her family was still recovering from the 1910 forest fire that had destroyed their house, chickens, mill, and all the cut lumber and railroad ties waiting to be hauled. The family escaped with only a little furniture, some clothes, and some bedding that was drying on the clothes line when the fire broke out. Lucy was two years old at the time and remembered being carried down a road toward the river by a man helping the family flee the fire.

After Lucy finished first grade, her father moved the family sawmill to Edgeware in northern Spokane County, and she was forced to change schools. Since there was no school at Edgeware, her parents rented an apartment in Newport so their four daughters could stay together and attend school in town. Her mother was not able to move with her daughters because she was needed at the sawmill, so the older daughters took care of the younger ones. Second grader Lucy was terribly homesick for the entire year and a half the girls lived in Newport. By 1917, Lucy's oldest sister, Maude, had married and was able to cook for her father's crew which left her mother free to take care of her three younger daughters while they continued their educations in the area.

Katherine Burley

In 1917, Katherine Burley was the second of three children to attend the Jore School as a first grader and attended all eight grades at the school. Just prior to enrolling, she had moved with her parents, Andrew and Ida, and sisters, Bernice and Josephine, to a ranch near Newport where they lived until she graduated from eighth grade in 1925. Her parents were advocates of education and Andrew Burley was elected to the school board in March 1920 and re-elected in March 1924.[16]

The Burley family ranch, a mile from the school, had once been a sawmill. Katherine's father sold some lumber in Newport in addition to raising cows and chickens. A large garden provided plenty of chores for the girls.

Katherine and her sisters had to walk up and down a very hilly cross-country path to school, often walking uphill to and from school. In the winter, their father plowed the path, as best he could, with his sled so the snow would not be too deep for their short legs. Often, the girls saw fresh bear or coyote tracks following their path.

The Burley farm wasn't productive, and Ida wanted her girls to have an education past the eighth grade, so when Katherine finished the Jore School in 1925, the Burley women left the ranch and rented a house in Newport where the girls enrolled in high school. The excellent education at the Jore School made the transition to Newport High School easy. Their father worked for the Spokane Post Office during the week and returned to his family in Newport on weekends.

After the two older girls graduated from high school,

the family moved to Cheney where Katherine continued her education at Cheney Normal School, and her father commuted daily from Spokane to Cheney by car. Once Katherine finished the normal school, the family moved to Spokane where she became a teacher.

Ivan Troyer

Like Katherine Burley, Ivan Troyer attended all eight grades at the Jore School. He enrolled as a first grader in 1921 and successfully passed his eighth grade examination in 1929. During at least one school year, Ivan recorded perfect attendance, a considerable achievement considering the weather, his mode of transportation, and the distance he had to travel. Ivan lived four miles from school and remembered his first day very clearly:

> "I rode to school by myself and put my horse in the barn and kids began showing up. I was having a good time playing with them when somebody rang a bel,l and the kids all ran off and left me. I got my horse out of the barn and rode home."[17]

When Ivan's parents, Ira and Maude, realized he needed some help getting started at school, they arranged with the Burley family to have Ivan ride his horse to the Burley farm and walk the last mile to school with the three Burley girls. He even sat in a desk with Katherine until he became adjusted to school. Later, Ivan rode the four miles every day, getting there early enough to put his horse, Betty, in the barn and feed it before the bell rang.

Ivan became very comfortable at school. Being something of a daredevil, he once rode his horse right into the schoolroom to amuse his teacher, Madelyne Black. During his last years at Jore, he sometimes rode his bicycle. One day he took his bicycle down to visit classmate Twylah Giem and gave her a ride on the handlebars. As they were riding down a farm road, he hit a rock and the two went flying over the handlebars and landed on the road.[18]

Ivan graduated from the Jore School in 1929 and enrolled at Newport High School. After one year at Newport High, a bull left Ivan's father with an arm injury. The family then moved to Metaline Falls where Ira worked in the mines and Ivan finished high school and met his wife, Rose.

The couple was married on October 8, 1938. Ivan owned a machine shop in Newport for seven years and worked at the shipyards in Vancouver, Washington, during World War II.

Twylah Giem

Twylah Giem entered the sixth grade at Jore School in 1925 when she was 13 years old. Her late enrollment was due to her family having lived in rural Montana where there were no schools. Their Montana farm was eight miles from Dodson and 18 miles from Malta. Eventually, her mother rented a small place in Dodson and her two children Twylah, eight and sister Mabel, eleven, began in the same first grade class.[19]

The Giem family had attempted to raise oats, wheat, barley, and flax in Montana, but insects and bad weather ruined their crops year after year. When they arrived on their new land in Pend Oreille County, Twylah remembered helping her mother prepare logs for their new barn by sorting the good logs from those burned in the 1910 fire. Her mother built most of the family's house while her father worked at the Diamond Mill in Newport for $3.20 a day. He stayed in town during the week, and on Saturday nights, her mother would travel the fourteen miles round-trip to pick-up her husband and repeat the trip Sunday night. The routine lasted every week for two years until the family purchased a car in 1927. Until they finished their log barn and frame house, the Giems rented a house from their nearest neighbors, the Pratts, who were gone for the winter. The family's new house was five miles from the school, and the sisters often journeyed to school on horseback.

Twylah's favorite subjects were Art and Geography. She remembered that she could, without looking at a map, draw all the states, including Washington State with all its counties, cities and rivers.

Once in the sixth grade, Twylah acted out in class.

Photo courtesy of Pend Oreille County Historical Society.

Jore School class photo, 1926. Front row left to right: Ardis Holt, Arlie Holt, Juanita Garrison. Middle row: Bernice Guerin, Lavern Peterson, Odessa Guerin, Virgil Jore. Top row: Walter Smith, Grace Holt, Mabel Giem, Twylah Giem, Catherine Guerin, and Ivan Troyer.

Her teacher, Miss Ruth Johnson, told her to stay after school. Twylah talked to her sister Mabel just before school was dismissed and asked her to bring both of their horses up to the porch. When the children were dismissed for the day, Twylah asked Miss Johnson for permission to use the outhouse, then ran outside, jumped on her horse, and rode home.

Her seventh and eight grade "classes" were quite small—only her and the teacher's (Miss Madelyne Black) brother, Donald.

Twylah graduated from the Jore School in 1928 and transferred to Newport High. The first day at her new school was a bit overwhelming. She missed half her classes because she forgot she had to change rooms and had trouble finding them. During her first year at Newport High School, she lived with the Muehalthaler family in town and took care of their children and home in exchange for room and board. Later she stayed with two of her married sisters. On the weekends, she rode home with her father who was still working at the Diamond Mill during the week and commuting to the farm on the weekends. When the Jore School was consolidated into the Newport School District, a school bus came for the students, but it was still a two-mile walk from Twylah's family home to the bus stop.

Since Twylah started school late, she and her teacher, Madelyne Black, were nearly the same age and remained friends until Madelyne's death. Twylah credited her teachers for giving her academic encouragement and motivating her to continue her education. As a result, she was the only child in her family to finish the eighth grade and graduate from high school.

Ron Geaudreau

In 1929, the school's last year of operation, Ron Geaudreau came to the Jore School as a third grader and his mother, Stella, was hired as a teacher. Because

Jore students arriving at school in 1926. Left to Right: Juanita Garrison, Twylah Giem, Walter Smith, Ivan Troyer, and Virgil Jore.

his mother had no babysitter and Ron's father, Frank, worked when and where he could, Ron began his schooling at the Colockum School, near Wenatchee, Washington, when he was only five years old. During his second grade year, the family moved to the Lost Creek School, about 10 miles south of Ione, Washington. After his third grade year in the Jore School, he returned to Lost Creek for the rest of his elementary school career.[20]

Ron and his mother enjoyed the Jore School; it was close to Newport and by walking out to the road on Friday afternoons, they could get a bus or hitch a ride home. On Saturday afternoons, it was not difficult to get to the silent pictures shown at the Newport Movie Theater. Ron also liked the treatment he got from Grandma Jore who gave him cream to drink because he was so skinny.

After passing the eighth grade exam, Ron Geaudreau enrolled at North Central High School in Spokane and easily made the adjustment from a school with ten students to one of 2,000. After graduating in 1935, he became a dental technician and instructor at Bates College in Tacoma.

The Smith Boys

The Smith family sent four sons, Marion, Percy, Clarence, and Walter to the Jore School. Their mother, Prudence, was very strict and insisted that her sons attend school. At least one of the boys was enrolled each year from 1918 until 1929 with all four boys attending during the 1917-1918 school year.[21]

Norman Smith and his wife Prudence, who was 18 years his junior, supported their family by means of the family farm. They raised cows, pigs, chickens, alfalfa and planted an acre of potatoes each year. Prudence milked the cows and made butter that was sold at Owens Grocery Store in Newport. Any extra cream was sent to a creamery. During winter, the family cut ice from the surface of Diamond Lake and stored it in their icehouse. Surrounded by sawdust, the ice lasted through the summer. The boys remembered turning the crank of the ice cream maker every Sunday during the hot weather.

Like other one-room schoolhouse students, the lard pails the Smith boys carried figured prominently in their school memories. They got in trouble when they lost them and occasionally used them for defense. One day they started on their way to school only to find the road was flooded. Afraid of missing school, they threw their lunch buckets on the ground and built a raft. When it was completed, they grabbed their buckets and boarded the craft, which sank immediately. Their lunch buckets went down the creek; they didn't make it to school, and they found themselves in deep trouble with their mother. Earlier, when the Smith boys first arrived at the school, they had to prove how tough they were, and the oldest boy, Marion, used his lunch bucket to clout another boy and establish his place in the playground hierarchy.

When the boys finished their education at the Jore School, they moved to Newport for high school and lived in a second floor apartment. To enhance their quality of life, they ate as much food as they could get from the home economics classes and tapped into free electricity by running a wire to the power line running in the street.

Photo courtesy of Smith Family.

The Smith Family: back row, George, Clarence, and Percy; middle row, Prudence and Norman; front row, Walter.

One-Room Education

The basic education in the one-room school provided a good foundation for high school and beyond. Prescribed curricula, visits from the county superintendent, and the eighth grade examination provided quality control in the schools. Parents made sacrifices for this education and expected their children to do well in school. This combination of forces allowed a good deal of learning to take place, even when very few educational resources were available. For a few years beginning in 1912, the school served as a model rural schoolhouse for Cheney Normal School. The rural school department of the Cheney Normal School was organized on September 1, 1908. Its object was "to demonstrate just what improvements may be made in our rural schools in general by the proper application of the right methods, by correlating and alternating the work, and by placing in charge a teacher who has the natural adaptability and special training for this particular kind of work."[21]

Eventually five rural demonstration schools were formed. The first was in Spokane County about three miles from Cheney on the electric train line. The other four were located in Adams, Lincoln, Stevens and Pend Oreille Counties. Every future teacher in the normal school who was not in the rural school program was required to observe in the Spokane County School while those in the program were sent to the other four schools. Education within the walls of the one-room schoolhouse was the same across the nation. Children worked quietly and independently at their desks while the teacher called one group of children at a time to the recitation bench. At the bench, they recited their lessons and were given assignments to complete at their desks. The teacher moved quickly from group to group and subject to subject, taking only recess and lunch breaks.

Students usually ranged in age from six to thirteen, but there were exceptions. Factors such as prior education, family obligations on the farm, and severe winters affected the school careers of students. Each fall they went back to school and picked up where they had left off.[22]

Jore School days began at 9:00 A.M. and ended at 4:00 P.M. A one-hour lunch break and two fifteen-minute recess breaks were allowed during the day. In the winter, recesses were shortened so students could finish their school day at 3:30 P.M. and reach home before dark.[23]

Days at the Jore School began by marching outside to raise and salute the flag. The students returned indoors and began with singing class. Each student had a song book from which different songs were chosen each day. Normally, students sang and the teacher accompanied on the piano. Doris Bloodgood, teacher at the Hoisington School, couldn't play the piano, so she used a small record player and some old records to teach music appreciation.[24] After the class finished singing, some teachers assigned different students to give an oral report on current events reported in the local small weekly news magazine.[25] Roll call, which might normally follow these introductory exercises was seldom taken at the rural schools because teachers knew the children so well.

During the school day, each grade level was called up separately. A small one-room school did not always have a child in each grade. For instance, there might be three fifth graders in a school but no students in fourth grade. This was obviously the case at the Jore School when Miss Blanche Hill taught. Her "Program of Daily Exercises," dated May 19, 1912, shows a day at the Jore School.

9:00-9:05	Opening Exercises
9:05-9:20	1st Grade Reading
9:20-9:35	2nd Grade Reading
9:35-9:45	3rd Grade Reading
9:45-9:55	5th Grade Reading
9:55-10:05	6th Grade Reading
10:05-10:20	7th & 8th Grade Reading
10:20-10:30	6th Grade History
10:30-10:45	Recess
10:45-11:10	1st, 2nd, 3rd Grade Arithmetic
11:10-11:20	7th Grade History
11:20-11:30	8th Grade History
11:30-11:45	5th & 6th Grade Arithmetic
11:45-12:00	7th & 8th Grade Arithmetic
12:00-1:00	Lunch
1:00-1:10	Writing
1:10-1:25	1st Grade Reading
1:25-1:40	2nd Grade Reading
1:40-1:50	3rd Grade Reading
1:50-2:00	5th Grade Language
2:00-2:10	6th Grade Language
2:10-2:20	7th Grade Grammar
2:20-2:30	8th Grade Grammar
2:30-2:45	Recess
2:45-3:10	Spelling Classes
3:10-3:25	7th & 8th Grade Physiology
3:25-3:35	5th Grade Geography
3:35-3:50	6th & 8th Grade Geography
3:50-4:00	7th Grade Geography[26]

The following is an account of Ron Geaudreau's school day:

> "Let's say I was in the first grade. I had to read and so I went up right next to the teacher's desk and I would read out loud to her and I would face her so that my back was to the other students and my voice wouldn't carry. After I read, she would give me my math problems and I would return to my seat to do them. Then another kid would come up. We knew almost to the minute when we would have to be up. If someone else was in the same grade, 2 or 3 students might come up at the same time. If I was in a group, she would stop me and someone else would take a turn reading. Then we would be called up for math. Some would write their math lessons on the board and others did their work on paper. Chalk and books were provided. Parents were expected to provide paper and pencils. I remember that one really poor family would write real lightly on the paper and then erase it after the teacher saw it. This family had thirteen kids."[27]

The methods used in the one-room school were dictated by the daily schedule set forth by the Pend Oreille Country Superintendent that allowed very little time for instruction of any one grade or individual. Teachers called out "rise and pass" and students filed up to the recitation bench by grade level and subject matter, and the teachers tested the student's level of knowledge

on a subject either orally or in writing. [28] Once the
teacher assessed their progress, he or she gave direct
instruction where needed and explained the next day's
work. That grade then sat down, and the next group
was asked to "rise and pass."

Students studied silently when not reciting. Some
students learned by listening to the recitations of other
classes and others devoured books in the tiny school
library. A great favorite of some of the students was the
dictionary with its pictures of animals, birds, and a double
page of national flags. Students could find a flag in the
dictionary and then find the corresponding country on
the roll down maps.[29]

Competitive learning games, such as spelling and
arithmetic bees, were welcome changes for students and
teacher alike. In math races, two students stood beside
their desks as the teacher recited or showed flash cards
inscribed with an addition, subtraction, or multiplication
problem. The student with the quickest correct answer
moved on to the next desk and the loser sat down. The
next student stood up and "raced" with the previous
winner. The object of the game was to defeat everyone
in the class. Sometimes the game lasted for several laps
around the room, and usually, the older students were
allowed, and encouraged, to help the younger ones.

Memorization was an important part of the education in all schools. Teachers were encouraged to give exercises in composition and declamation, including memorization of choice selections and quotations. In addition to working quietly while others recited, students were expected to arrive at school on time, obey the school rules, and be respectful to the teacher.

There were five rules for pupils in Pend Oreille County:

1. Every pupil shall be punctual and regular in attendance, obedient to all rules of the school, diligent in study, respectful and obedient to teachers and kind and obliging to schoolmates.
2. Willful disobedience, habitual truancy, vulgarity or profanity, the use of tobacco, stealing, the carrying of deadly weapons, the carrying or using of dangerous playthings, shall constitute good cause for suspension or expulsion from school.
3. As soon as dismissed, pupils shall leave the school premises and go directly to their homes. Loitering on the way to and from school is positively forbidden.
4. Pupils shall give attention to personal neatness and cleanliness, and any who fail in this respect may be sent home to be prepared properly for school.
5. Pupils shall not be detained more than forty minutes after the regular hour for dismissal.[30]

Students were expected to pay attention to their work and to the teacher at all times. Jore students had very little to distract them from outside the windows. Few vehicles traveled the road in front of the school. But whenever a horse drawn carriage or motorized vehicle went by, everyone in the class couldn't help look out and see what was going by. According to Ivan Troyer, "We knew we weren't supposed to look up but we just had to."[31]

Students were strongly encouraged to behave when the county superintendent paid the mandated twice-yearly visit. These were teacher evaluation sessions in which superintendents recorded the number of students in each grade and rated the teacher in the categories of methods, discipline, habits and manners, and county superintendents sometimes made presentations during their visits and sometimes took the opportunity to act as master teacher, grilling students and teachers alike.

The curriculum at one-room schools was prescribed by the county school district and was designed to prepare students to pass the eighth grade examination. It included reading, language, arithmetic, spelling, penmanship, geography, history, current events, literature, and physical education.

The eighth grade exam was administered by teachers or a proctor, who was often a school board member. An official would bring in the test and stay until the students completed it. He or she would then seal and send it to the county superintendent who then recorded the grades of every student in the county who had taken the examination.[32] Administration of the test took two days usually in January, May, and June in Pend Oreille County. In order to pass the test, students had to receive a score of no less than 60 percent in every subject, with the exception of grammar and arithmetic which had to be at least 80 percent, and their overall average in all subjects could be no lower than 80 percent. Students' writing was graded on a manuscript submitted with the test results. In addition to earning the minimum scores, no pupil received a certificate without reading one or more books adopted for the pupils' reading circle.[33]

Teaching to the test was common. Teachers picked up extra copies of the test and let students take sections in the sixth and seventh grades to get them ready. County superintendent's records of eighth grade examinations showed that some students took the entire test or sections of the test early. Ivan Troyer took parts of the examination in sixth, seventh, and eighth grades.

After he passed a section, he no longer had to take that subject. In the eighth grade, he passed all sections but one and traveled to Newport to take that section in June.[34]

Teachers encouraged their students to take the test, but some refused, thinking they would need no further education. However, a student who successfully passed the examination was entitled to enter any high school in the state. Students from the Jore School went on to work in many professions.

Life at the Jore School was not all work. Recess and lunch were always welcome breaks in the day. Children often raced and played tag or baseball during morning and afternoon recess. Girls jumped ropes and played tiddley winks. Once, Ron Geaudreau and his classmates built a cabin in the woods next to the play yard. The small house didn't have a door or a window, so the children climbed in through the top.[35]

Boys had their own set of rules on the playground. Being a country boy in a one-room schoolhouse demanded more than just being a student. "Back then a little country boy who didn't have a jack knife and slingshot just wasn't properly dressed," remembered Ron Geaudreau.[36] Whenever a new boy moved into a new school, he had to fight to determine his place in the playground hierarchy. The newcomer began by wrestling the littlest boy and then one of his own size. He kept fighting bigger and bigger boys until he got beat, usually when he yelled "uncle." Once his place was established, he was left alone.

At recess, "Pom Pom Pullaway" was a popular game on the playground. In Pom Pom Pullaway, two lines were drawn in the dirt about 50 to 100 yards apart. One player was chosen to be "it." The rest of the children lined up behind one of the lines. The "it" player stood between the children and the other line, facing them. "It" signaled the players to begin running toward the other line by saying. "Pom pom pull away, all the runners run away!" If the "it" player tapped a runner three times on the back, they become a catcher. The game continued until all the students were caught. The last one caught became the new "it."

When there was snow on the ground, children played "Fox and Geese." The game began with a circle made in the snow. The middle was the "safe zone" and only one person was allowed in at a time. A student, the "fox", chased the other children, who were the geese, and the person caught by the fox became the new fox.[37]

Snow brought sleds to the Jore School, and when Ruth Johnson taught during the 1926-1927 school year, she brought her skis and let the students ski down the hill. Once, before any of them knew how to ski, the children convinced the biggest girl, Catherine Guerin, to get on the front of the skis. One or two of the other girls stood behind her and the trio flew down the hill. They hit a gully about halfway down, went tumbling, and survived to try again.

Next to recess, lunch time was the best part of the day. Most carried lunches to school in lard or Union Leader tobacco tins with handles. Bill Shukle's father smoked enough tobacco to supply all of the children in the family with cans for lunch.[38] Coming up with nutritious lunches was a challenge even for farm families because most of the food was harvested for sale to support the family. The lunch bucket usually contained a sandwich or a boiled egg, and sometimes a piece of fruit, cake, or cookie. Few sandwiches were filled with meat or cheese. Most students remembered bringing jam, mustard, plum butter, or peanut butter and jelly sandwiches. Some children even brought sandwiches made with dark Karo syrup. They tasted good, but were messy to eat.

Most one-room schools did not serve hot lunch, but in a few the teacher cooked soup, stew, chili, or hot cocoa on the stove during the cold winter months. At the Hoisington School near Elk, Washington, the teacher, Doris Bloodgood was also the cook. She provided hot lunches for the children from October through May. The community financed these meals by sponsoring box socials and taking up collections at the dances held in the schoolhouse. And when Doris visited her family home almost every weekend, she would fix up a pot of chili or some other meal for the following week for the class.

Other teachers received donations to keep hot lunch programs going. Mary Mele Mauro cooked for the children in her class at the Buckeye School in northeast

Photo courtesy of Pend Oreille County Historical Society.

Ruth Johnson on the steps of the teacherage in 1926.

Spokane County. Like Doris, Mary went home on weekends and her father, a Spokane grocer, gave her stew meat, and she organized committees of children to bring vegetables so they could cook stew on the classroom stove.[39] Stella Geaudreau did not cook lunch for her students, but they did make a hot lunch once a year. On this special day, everyone brought a vegetable or a piece of meat, and she put it in a stew pot on the stove and let it cook all morning, her son and student Ron recalled, "The smell of that simmering stew was wonderful."[40]

Students left their cold lunches in the cloakrooms during the fall months but had to bring them near the stove during the coldest months of the year, or they would be frozen by lunchtime. On the very coldest days students would sit around the heater and eat their lunches. Some teachers had lunch games. Louise Ranek remembered a game that started with the youngest child saying, "On my way to school I saw," and then they would describe it in detail what they saw without telling what it was. The first one to guess correctly would be the next one to describe what he or she saw.[41] In good weather, students took their lunches outside to eat.

Water hauled from pumps on the playground, nearby houses, streams, or wells was also served during lunch time. The water was kept in a barrel with a spigot on the outside.[42] At some schools, students drank from a common dipper. In others where the teacher was more fastidious, each student brought a cup or glass from home and labeled it with their name. Some schools had the students buy collapsible cups for their water while in others they fashioned individual cups from plain paper.

Jore School Teachers

Teachers of one-room schools taught on many different kinds of certificates. To earn a First Class certificate, a teacher candidate had to earn at least 1170 credits out of 1300 possible on the examination and could not fall below 90 percent. For a Second Class certificate a candidate was required to earn a total of 800 credits and not fall under 80 percent. A Third Class certificate was earned with a total of 700 credits and a minimum of 70 percent. Before 1918, Washington State teachers could teach on First Class, Second Class, Third Class and Lifetime Certificates. Teachers earned their teaching certificates by attending colleges, normal schools, and taking examinations. The examination covered thirteen subject areas:

> Orthography, Arithmetic (mental and written), Grammar, United States History and Constitution, Theory and Practice, State School Law and Constitution, Physiology, Geography, Reading, Writing, Algebra, Physics, and Literature.

In 1918, several changes were made in the state teacher certification requirements. No new First, Second or Third Class certificates were issued after September 1, 1918. Second and Third Class Certificates could be renewed with a prescribed amount of experience and coursework at an institution of higher education. One semester of coursework was required for the Second Class certificate renewal and an entire year of coursework was required for renewal of the First Class certificate.

After 1918, Permanent Certificates, Second Class Elementary Certificates, First Class Elementary Certificates and Life Certificates were issued. As before, teachers could earn these certificates with a combination of course work and testing.

Each year, rural teachers attended a week-long teacher institute to update their teaching skills. In some parts of the country, the institutes were scheduled to allow the students to work in the fall harvest. The institutes followed a regular daily pattern. Each day began with roll call followed by group singing. Following the opening exercises, experts from normal schools, colleges, and universities presented sessions on educational topics until the assembly dismissed at noon for an hour break. The institute reconvened each day at 1:00 P.M. with a second roll call, another song, and sessions lasting until 5:00 P.M. Dinner was followed by additional sessions.

Sessions were designed to give teachers insights into their work and to keep them abreast of the latest educational topics. Sessions included "The Relations of Teacher to Community," "The Problem of Attendance," and "Music that Children Like," as well as sessions on Grammar, Language, Mathematics, and History. Evening programs were a mixture of musical and literary programs and lectures from professors.

As the only employee of the one-room school, teachers served as janitor, cook, principal, counselor, and secretary. Often, teachers arrived early on cold mornings to build fires and stayed late planning, correcting papers, and banking the stove for the next day. Their teaching ability was judged by the number of students who passed the eighth grade examination, as well as students' performances at programs and contests. While the county superintendent came twice a year to observe the classroom, the local school board kept teachers under much closer scrutiny.

Married women were hired to teach in one-room schools when they were forbidden from teaching in larger towns. They often had to live away from their families or bring their children with them as they taught.

More than 30 teachers taught at the Jore School in its 37-year history and their lives mirrored those of teachers in other one-room school districts. Jore School teachers taught classes with as many as 36 students and as few as 10. The size of the school population rose and fell with the fortunes of the area. One family moving in or out of the area could change the school census by four or five children. Over the years, teachers' salaries ranged from $40.00 to $125.00 each month, with some receiving an additional $2.00 a month for janitorial work. Teachers who stayed with the Jore family had a private room in the house and had a walk of only about a quarter mile.

Teachers who boarded with the Jore family included Ella McDowell, who taught at the school from 1911-1913 and Julia Nagle Johnson who taught during 1919-1920. In a letter to her family, Julia wrote:

> "My second assignment was at the Jore School, about 8 miles out of Newport on the Deer Valley Road. It was considered to have a venerable history, having been started in the early 1900s. A sawmill, running in the Jore Meadow, brought a lot of families whose children came to my school. I had a well-filled schoolroom comprising all eight grades. I boarded with kindly little Mrs. Jore who made life pleasant with her generosity, her fatima and her Jul-kaka. Family names that I recall are: Jore, Marin, Burley, Oakes, Bloom, Smith, and Mitchell."[43]

The first teacher to occupy the teacherage at the Jore School was Mary Headrick, who taught in 1920-21 and 1923-24 school years. Before the teacher's cottage was built, she commuted on horseback daily from her nearby farm. County records show the year that she commuted to the school, she was the highest paid teacher in the history of the school making $125.00 per month. The reason is unclear, but it is speculated it is due of her long commute. When she returned to the school after another teaching job in Washington State in 1922-23, she signed a contract for $115.00, and in 1923-24, her salary dropped to only $100.00 per month.[44]

The last three Jore School teachers, Ruth Johnson, Madelyne Black, and Stella Geaudreau, all lived in the teacher's cottage and all earned $115.00 a month for teaching and $2.00 for doing the janitorial work.

Ruth Johnson came to the school in 1926 and was remembered for sharing with the children both her skis and the mumps which she caught from her brother during one of her weekends at home.

Madelyne Black taught for the next two years. Her brother, Donald, came to the Jore School as a student and stayed with her in the teacherage. During her tenure at the Jore School, she had an operation on her foot and had to be out of school for two weeks. Since there were no substitute teachers, her mother, a teacher, substituted for her in the classroom.

Stella Geaudreau followed Madelyne Black and taught during the last year of operation, 1928-29. She received her teaching certificate from Ellensberg Normal School and was issued a lifetime certificate after 27 months of teaching. Stella owned a home in Newport but, since married women were not allowed to teach in city school districts, she could only teach in one-room schools.

Teaching usually turned out to be more difficult than young teachers anticipated. The reality of the first day of teaching is best told by a teacher who had been a pupil in a one-room schoolhouse in 1911 and 1912 and who returned to another as a teacher.

> "On my first day of school, I returned home to announce that I would someday be a teacher because all a teacher did was ask questions and the children had to answer them.
>
> On my first day of teaching, this life-long illusion self-destructed in 30 seconds. Much to my surprise, when 42 question marks looked me square in the eye, I found that the teacher also had to know all the answers and how to make a fire in a coal or wood stove, and how to prepare an adequate lunch, and how to provide entertainment for all sorts of occasions,

and how to crowd all the subjects into one day!

I learned that in a rural school, kindergarten through eighth grade, I would have to be nurse, doctor, mother, counselor, cook, custodian, babysitter, referee, and diplomat living on promises.

On that first day, I was amazed at the size of my pupils, especially the boys; I wasn't sure whether to date them or teach them, but I remembered that my contract specifically mentioned teaching, so I set about my task. There followed one of the longest days of my life. The clock literally stood still. It gave very little boost to my already deflated ego when I overheard one of the six-foot boys whisper, 'She'll never make it!'" [45]

School children played pranks even when their teachers were good classroom managers. Boys who sat behind girls with braids were sorely tempted to dip them into their inkwells and frequently gave in to the temptation. An unsuspecting teacher sometimes found a snake or frog in her desk.

Even though discipline was important for the one-room school teacher, it was only a part of his or her duties as defined in the rules and regulations for teachers in Washington State in 1912.

Rules and Regulations Adopted by the State Board of Education, 1912

1. The teachers in the public schools of this state shall follow the prescribed course of study and enforce the rules and regulations of the State Board of Education; shall keep records, use blanks and render reports according to instructions.

2. Teachers shall be held responsible for the care of all school property entrusted to them; shall frequently inspect the same and promptly report to the district clerk any damage it may have received.

3. Each teacher shall prepare a program of daily exercises, a copy of which shall be posted in a conspicuous place in the school room.

4. Teachers shall exercise watchful care over the conduct and habits of the pupils while under their jurisdiction.

5. Teachers shall maintain strict order and discipline in their schools at all times. Any neglect of this requirement shall be considered good cause for dismissal. Corporal punishment may be resorted to when it becomes necessary to the preservation of proper discipline. No cruel or unusual punishment shall be inflicted; and no teacher shall administer punishment on or about the head of any pupil.

6. In the case of misconduct or insubordination, when the teacher deems it necessary for the good of the school, he may suspend a pupil, and shall immediately notify the directors of the district thereof for further action, and shall

send a copy of said notice to the parents or guardians of the child.

7. Every public school teacher shall give vigilant attention to the temperature and ventilation of the schoolroom and shall see that the atmosphere of the room is frequently changed.

8. Teachers shall have the right, and it shall be their duty, to direct and control within reasonable limits the studies of the pupils: provided, that all pupils shall receive instruction in the branches included in the prescribed course of study.

9. The use of tobacco in any form or place by a teacher is discountenanced, and the use of alcoholic stimulants in any form or place as a beverage is prohibited. The use of tobacco or any other narcotic on the school premises by a teacher shall work a forfeiture of his certificate.

10. The teacher shall make an estimate of the worth of each pupil's work in the several subjects as often as once every two months. This estimate shall be based upon the pupil's daily work, together with such tests as the teacher may deem it advisable to give during the period.

11. At the close of every term of school the teacher shall thoroughly examine, in all necessary branches, all pupils whose work has not been satisfactory and shall leave in the school register a statement of the work completed by each pupil in each subject. He shall also leave a record of the deportment of each pupil.

12. Teachers shall require excuses from the parents or guardians of pupils, either in person or by

written note, in all case of absence, tardiness or dismissal before the close of school, and no excuse shall be deemed valid except that of sickness. Excuses for absence shall be placed in the hands of the attendance officer, and it shall be the duty of said attendance officer to investigate thoroughly each case and enforce the provisions of the law regarding thereto.

13. An attendance of less than one hour at any half-day's session shall not be counted by the teacher in taking his or her annual report.

14. Teachers are enjoined to encourage exercises in composition and declamation, including memorization of choice selections and quotations. In the preparation of programs for rhetoricals, teachers shall use every effort to secure selections of a high literary character.

15. Teachers are required to be at their respective schoolrooms at least thirty minutes before the time of opening school in the morning and fifteen minutes before the opening of school in the afternoon.

16. Teachers are required to make due preparation daily for their duties, such preparation to include attendance upon teachers' meetings and other professional work contributing to efficient school service, which may be required by the superintendent, principal, or board of directors.[46]

Not only were teachers forbidden to smoke and drink, but their personal lives were also under scrutiny with harsh results. Some districts were a little over zealous in enforcing the rules. In St. John, Washington, a teacher was riding her horse straddle, rather than side-saddle, on the main street, and when she passed the president of the school board, she was fired on the spot.[47] Mary Mauro was also a witness to the power of the local school board. One day she went to her school in Colbert, Washington and the door was locked without any explanation. [48]

Special Events at the Jore School

Schoolhouses were also used outside of the school day for evening programs and non-school events. Former pupils remember Christmas and spring programs, as well as the end of the year potluck. For some communities, schoolhouses served as community centers after hours and provided the setting for Saturday night dances and meetings of the literary society, even the occasional revival. The Jore Schoolhouse, like others, was the scene of this kind of activity, drawing entire families by wagon, foot, and horseback.

During school sponsored programs, each student would stand and recite or sing a song or take part in a skit. When the official program was finished, a dessert buffet would be laid out on the teacher's desk with hot coffee. It was often midnight before the families began the journey back home.

The Christmas program was always a special event in the country school. The children performed skits and memorized holiday pieces. Parents and teachers joined them in singing familiar Christmas carols and Santa Claus would come and give each child a trinket. An orange was considered a special treat.

Photo courtesy of Pend Oreille County Historical Society.

Jore School end of the year picnic, 1927. The woman standing in front wearing the black dress is Miss Madelyne Black.

At the end of the school year picnic, entire families would come to the school and bring food to share. On these occasions, too, there would often be recitations or skits, as well as baseball, three-legged races, and other traditional picnic activities.

Weekend dances were held in local one-room schoolhouses. Round dances, square dances, the schottische, and polka were particularly popular. Since babysitters were unheard of at the time, entire families came to the dances that traditionally began at 8:00 P.M. Young unmarried men also came to get acquainted with the young girls.

School desks were pushed to the side of the room and covered with coats, scarves, and lap robes. As the evening wore on, sleepy children climbed up between the coats and fell asleep. More that one child remembered waking up when a tired dancer sat down for a rest or waking up with another child's foot in his or her face.

The music was provided by local musicians. Fiddlers, piano, guitar, harmonica, horn players, and drummers were all welcome. The musicians played until midnight when the teacher's desk was turned into a buffet table holding a potluck supper of sandwiches and cakes. Coffee that had been heating on the stove from the beginning of the dance was ready to serve by midnight.

Blanche Hill, teacher during, 1911-1912. These souvenirs were given out on the last day of school as a memento of the year.

Dancing continued after the meal and traditionally went on until daybreak. Families often drove home as the sun rose, arriving just in time to do the morning milking. In cold weather, those who brought automobiles often found them impossible to start and were forced to hitch a ride in a horse and buggy, to the delight of those who did not own a car.

Dances were announced and reported on by the local newspapers. Usually they were described as successful, well-attended, and a wonderful diversion from the isolated pioneer life. However, there were exceptions. At the Hoisington School, one of the dancers drank a little too much and left the building by diving out of a closed window. The community pitched in and the window was immediately repaired.[49]

Another example of a schoolhouse dance gone wrong was reported in a local Eastern Washington newspaper in 1914.

> "In the early hours of the evening the dancing only occasionally showed objectionable features; but as morning drew near the dancing became fast and furious, and a certain abandonment crept in that was plainly noticeable. First one and then another of the Morrison School District people began to mutter against the character of the dancing.
>
> We do not know what name to give to the dance we saw Valentine night. It may have been the "bunny hug," the "grizzly bear," the "turkey trot" or the "tango;" but whatever it was, it looked decidedly suggestive to us. We feel sure it could have only a bad moral effect on the school children who were present and who looked on eagerly at the behavior of their elders. This is one good reason why some of us are determined that the dances hereafter shall be conducted in such a manner that a

man may bring his wife and children to them, or a young man come with his sister or his sweetheart and not feel embarrassed.

As a result of the shocking behavior of the dancers, the following rules are proposed:

1. The so-called "moonlight waltz" to be prohibited. It is felt that if there is anything to conceal in the semi-darkness of the dance we do not wish to encourage it, and if there is nothing to conceal we might as well have the lights turned up.
2. No walking more than three steps either way. More than that will be regarded as "ragging" and will not be tolerated.
3. Hereafter no dance shall take place without floor managers being appointed who will be held responsible to the taxpayers for the decent and moral conduct of the dance.
4. Men will not be allowed to hold their partners in the deathlike grip indulged in by so many at present.
5. Every third dance shall be a square dance.
6. Dance to close hereafter at 2:30 A.M.

One young man wanted to know what a fellow is to do when a young girl wanted to "rag." That is easily answered. Do not invite such girls to the Morrison dances; they are not wanted here. Neither are young men wanted who do not know how to behave properly at a dance."[50]

Schools were also the site for meetings of local literary societies. Literaries elected a president and a secretary and held events appropriate to the community. These organizations were mainly made up of any community member with an interest in the arts and organizing community activities. Some had loosely organized programs, but others presented debates, musical programs, dramatic readings, and mock trials. A particular favorite in the Columbia Basin of Washington was the mock wedding, where the part of the groom was played by the shortest woman present and the role of bride was filled by the tallest man.[51] Spelling bees and debates were common activities at literary societies. At times the debates got too wild and hard feelings developed over the competition. If the situation got too bad, school boards took the matter into their own hands.[52]

Pie socials and box socials were also popular and the proceeds were used to buy phonographs, records, books, art supplies, and other items that weren't included in the school budget.

At a box social, each woman packed a lunch and put it in a box decorated with ribbons and paper flowers or made to look like some other object, like an animal, mummy, house or barn. These decorated lunches would be auctioned off and the buyer of the lunch would get to sit and share it with the woman who had prepared and decorated it. Box socials were particularly popular when there were single men and women in the community. Younger brothers and sisters were sometimes paid to describe the wrapping of their sister's box to an interested young man. At pie socials, pies were put into specially decorated boxes and auctioned off in the same way.

Conclusion

America's one-room schoolhouses were created to provide rural children with the knowledge and skills necessary to participate in a democratic society. Their quality was upheld by a combination of inspections by county superintendents and the results of examinations given to departing eighth grade students. Local school boards and community members donated time and effort to support their local schools. When John and Betsy Jore donated the land to build a school to educate the 8 of their 14 children who survived early childhood, they were typical of homesteaders across the nation. Yet the impact of these schools surpassed their original mission. In some isolated locations they were the only public buildings for miles around. They served as meeting places, venues for entertainment, and places of worship.

The teachers hired by local school boards were models of self-sufficiency. There was no one else to depend on if things went wrong. They prepared the classroom, lit the fire, orchestrated all the daily activities and, more often than not, did the janitor work. They had very little personal privacy, living in the home of a nearby farmer or in a teacher's cottage on the school grounds. They served at the pleasure of the school board and could be asked to leave their positions without notice.

Many one-room schoolhouses disappeared during the consolidation movement. A few still stand abandoned in farmer's fields and on roadsides. Some have been wrapped into houses, grange halls, and churches. A few others have become living history museums where people of all ages can experience a significant part of the educational history of America.

The exterior of the Jore Schoolhouse, which now faces the education building on the Eastern Washington University campus, has been completely refurbished. Sitting on a new foundation and protected by a new roof, it awaits visitors who will come when the interior renovation is completed. School desks, books, inkwells, a wood stove, piano, slate blackboards, and other donated furnishings for the schoolhouse are safely stored in various buildings around the university.

When fund-raising is complete, the Cheney Normal

School Heritage center will open and embrace Eastern Washington University's heritage as a teacher preparation institution. It will be open for educational tours to school children and to the general public. The building will serve as a place where seminars and presentations are conducted related to the history and development of education in the Inland Empire. It will become a center for local and regional oral history where teachers, scholars and community members can share, record and preserve traditions, stories and records of the past; and a permanent location to house and display historical one-room schoolhouse artifacts.

Visitors to the schoolroom will relive the experiences of one-room schoolhouse pupils. Sitting in their desks with hands folded, they will listen while the teacher speaks, stand and recite when they are called upon, and work silently when they are called upon, and work silently when not reciting. They will complete assignments designed for students their age, and may be dismissed for recess where they will play organized games like "Pom Pom Pullaway" and "Fox and Geese." The Jore Schoolhouse will preserve an example of the setting where millions of rural American children gained the basic knowledge that served them for a lifetime. It will also recreate that expereince for the present and future generations.

Notes

[1] Ciphering was a term often used to describe arithmetic.

[2] G. Jones, "One Man, One School," <u>Perspective: A Magazine for Alumni and Friends of Eastern Washington University</u>, Volume 11, No. 4, (Fall 2000), pp. 5&6.

[3] Ibid., p. 6.

[4] Judy Rogers, director of development for the College of Education and Human Development, made a presentation to the marketing committee of the Spokane Teachers Credit Union in June 2000. At the end of the presentation, she mentioned that the President of the university had approved the acquisition of the one-room schoolhouse and that the Riley Lumber Company had donated the building. The idea of financing the school building was exciting to the board and its president Steve Dahlstrom, a graduate of EWU.

[5] <u>Cheney Free Press</u>, Cheney, Washington, August 24, 2000; <u>Spokesman-Review</u>, Spokane, Washington, August 16, 2000.

[6] Homestead proof-Testimony of Claimant. n.d. (approximately 1902), John Olsen Jore. The date is estimated from the statement that John Jore was 42 years old at the time he proved up on his homestead. He was born in 1860.

[7] Barbara Yonk and Jan Gellespie, personal interview, 5 October 2000

[8] Twylah Giem, personal interview.

[9] Rita Ritland, personal interview, 13 March 2001.

[10] Twylah Giem, personal interview.

[11] Catherine Ritland attended the school between 1918 and 1925. Julia Nagle Johnson, who taught at the school between 1919 and 1920 boarded with the Jore family. According to Catherine Ritland, Mary Headrick first commuted from her home and was the first teacher to live in the teacherage. That would put the date at 1922 or 1923. Mary Headrick taught at the school in 1920, 1922, and 1923.

[12] Ron Geaudreau, telephone interview, 19 December 2000.

[13] Ron Geaudreau, letter to Rita Seedorf, 1 February 2001.

[14] School Census records, Pend Oreille County, Washington State Archives, Eastern Region.

[15] Norma Wilson and Charles Woodard, eds. , <u>One Room Country School: South Dakota Stories</u>. Brookins, South Dakota: South Dakota Humaities Council, 1998.

[16] Giem interview.

[17] Geaudreau interview.

[18] Ritland interview: Ivan Troyer, personal interview 27 July 2001.

[19] Giem interview: Troyer interview.

[20] Bill Shukle, interview with Sandy Schiffner, 16 August 2001.

[21] Geaudreau interview.

[22] Geaudreau interview.

[23] Pend Oreille County Rules for teachers.

[24] Doris Bloodgood, personal interview, 3 July 2001.

[25] Wilson and Woodard.

[26] Faith Hill, Program of Daily Exercises, May 19, 1912.

[27] Geaudreau interview.

[28] Hubert Mills, personal interview, 18 October 2001.

[29] Wilson and Woodard.

[30] Rules for teachers, Newport Historical Society

[31] Troyer interview.

[32] Bloodgood interview.

[33] Pend Oreille County, record of Eighth Grade Examinations: Rules and Regulations adopted by the State Board of Education. Rules for Teachers 1912. Pend Oreille County Historical Society.

[34] Rules and Regulations adopted by the State Board of Education. Rules for Teachers 1912.

[35] Shukle interview.

[36] Geaudreau interview.

[37] Geaudreau interview

[38] Shukle interview.

[39] Mary Mauro, interviewed by Judy Rogers, 2000.

[40] Geaudreau interview.

[41] Wilson and Woodard.

[42] Geaudreau interview.

[43] Hand written note—Julia Nagle Johnson, Pend Oreille County Historical Society.

[44] Record of teacher contracts, Pend Oreille County, Washington State Archives.

45 Wilson and Woodard.

46 Pend Oreille County Rules for Teachers.

47 Miriam Trunkey, , ed. We got here from There: About schools in the vicinity of St. John, Washington 1883-1975., 1976.

48 Mary Mele Maura interview.

49 Bloodgood interview.

50 Neppel Record March 6, 1914.

51 Rita Seedorf, History of Moses Lake, 1992.

52 Jean Nipps Swaim, "The Era of the One Room Rural School in Cedar County, Missouri," Springfield, Missouri: Barnabas Publishing Services, 1999.

Jore School Enrollment 1912-1929

Allen, Donald 1919
Allen, Francis 1912
Allen, Ira 1912
Allen, James 1912
Allen Winnifred 1912
Applegate, Richard 1919
Applegate, Rose 1919
Baker, Albert 1915
Baker, Cora 1915
Baker, Earl 1915
Baird, Curtis 1922
Baird, Francis 1921-1929
Baird, Gardner 1920
Baird, Viola 1920
Beaubier, Robert 1928-1929
Berglund, Bertel 1915-1919
Beyersdorf, Donald 1912-1917
Beyersdorf, Glen 1913-1914,
    1916-1917
Beyersdorf, Guy 1912-1915
Beyersdorf, Orville 1917
Bloom, Carl 1918-1919
Bloom, Floyd 1915-1919
Bloom, Francis 1915-1919
Bloom, Harold 1915-1919
Bloom, Lawrence 1915-1919
Bloom, Raynold 1915-1919
Bloom, Roy 1915-1917

Burley, Bernice 1919-1924
Burley, Catherine 1919-1924
Burley, Josephine 1919-1924
Chambers, Ester 1917
Chambers, Gladys 1917
Chambers Ondas 1917
Chambers, Paul 1917
Chambers, Roy 1917
Clayton, Bertha 1916
Clayton, Beryl 1912-1915
Clayton, Harold 1912-1916
Clayton, Howard 1916
Clayton, Opal 1913-1916
Cline, Dorothy 1915
Cline, George 1913-1917
Cline, Homer 1913-1917
Coker, Ethel 1914
Cooney, Paul 1922
Cooney, Norman 1922
Coons, George 1920
Coons, Jewel 1920
Coons, Myrtle 1920
Coons, Pearl 1920
Coons, Royal 1920
Couch, Wayne 1922
Dyer, Jack 1917
Ellis, Hallene 1917
Ellis, Hazel 1917

Farsland, Margerie 1912
Farsland, Willie 1912
Fowler, Alice 1915-1920
Fowler, Fred 1914-1920
Fowler, Howard 1917-1920
Fowler, Ward 1919-1920
Garrison, Juanita 1926-1927
Gary, Henry/ Gay, Henry
1915/1913
Geaudreau, Ronald 1929
Geim, Irene 1926
Geim, Mabel 1926
Geim, Oscar 1926-1928
Geim, Twylah 1926-1928
Graham, Jennie 1912-1916
Graham, Katie 1912-1926
Graham, Lucy 1914-1916
Graham, Maude 1912-1916
Guerin, Bernice 1922-1927
Guerin, Catherine 1922, 1924-
1927
Guerin, Franses 1926-1927
Guerin, Odessa 1924-1927
Guerin, Ruth 1925-1927
Hatton, Cecil 1912-1917
Hatton, Dean 1913-1917
Hatton, Jean 1912
Hobbs, Nellie 1914-1915
Hobbs, Paul 1914-1915
Hoff, Elmer (Huff) 1912-1913
Holt, Ardis 1926
Holt, Arlie 1926
Holt, Grace 1926
Holt, Pearl 1926
Holt TIna 1926
Homes, Clara 1917
Homes, Edward 1917

Homes, Orlan 1917
House, Clara 1916
House, Edward 1916, 1918-
1920
House, Orlan 1916, 1918-1922
Howell, Lawrence 1912
Howell, Mary 1912
Howell, Mildred 1912
Johnson, Elaine 1923
Johnson, Lester 1917
Johnson, Mabel E 1915-1917
Jore, Annie 1912-1914, 1916
Jore, Mabel 1912, 1915
Jore, Virgil 1924-1927
Lanoue, Blanche 1918-1919
Lanoue, Edgar 1918
Lanoue, Jesse 1918-1921
Lanoue, Oscar 1918-1922
(Pemberton)
Lanoue, Tillie 1918-1922
(Pemberton)
Long, Cecil 1918-1919
Long, Ernest 1918-1919
Long, Leo 1918-1919
Long, Lloyd 1918-1919
Long, Willfred 1918-1919
Long, Willis 1918-1919
Marin, Arlie 1921
Marin Ester 1921-1922
Marin, George 1921-1922
Marin, Harvey 1921-1922
Marin, Marjorie 1921
Marin, Margaret 1922
Martin, Martha 1913
Martin Olivia 1913
McInnis, Arliedel 1929
McNeil, Robert 1928

Mitchell, Arthor 1912-1916,
    1918-1922
Mitchell, Clarence 1912-1920
Mitchell, Elsa 1913-
    1918(Elise, Alsa)
Mitchell, George 1912-1922
Mitchell, Harry 1912-1917
Mongan, Erla 1914-1921
Mongan, Ila 1914-1921
Moore, Clarence 1912-1915
Moore, Minnie 1912-1915
Moore, Wilbur 1920-1921
Moore, Willard 1920-1921
Moon, Leo 1915
Moser, Maryan 1924-1925
Oakes, Gladys 1920-1922
Oakes, Nettie 1920-1922
Overmeyer, Aubrey 1913
Overmeyer, Flora 1913
Overmeyer, Lora 1913
Overmeyer, Vivian 1921-1928
Oviatt, Ferressa 1917
Oviatt, Glen 1917
Oviatt, Theodore 1917
Pace, Chancy 1914-1915
Peterson, Clark 1913
Peterson Clarke 1921-1928
Peterson, LaVern 1922-1929
Peterson, Vivian 1921-1928
Ramey, Frank 1914
Ramey, Loach 1915
Rice, Everett 1915
Richardson, Harry 1916-1917
Robar, Edward 1914-1915
    (Ed)
Robar, Hattie 1914-1915
Robar, Ira 1914-1915 (Ivan)

Robar, Paul 1914-1915
Rombeck, Jacques 1921
Rombeck, Richard 1922
Rombeck Rose 1921-1922
Schimke, Albert 1917-1919
Schimke, Edwin 1917-1919
Schimke, Ernest 1919
Schmidt, Clara 1912, 1914
Schmidt, Tillia 1912, 1914
Schmidt, Tillie 1915, 1918,
    1920
Schmitt, Clara 1918
Schmitt, Ella 1927-1929
Schmitt, Mary 1927-1929
Scott, Joseph 1914
Scott, Rosa 1914
Scott, Walter 1914
Shaver, Allen 1913-1914, 1916
Shaver, Burton 1913-1916
Shaver, Edith 1914
Shaver, Edwin 1915
Shaver, Ella 1915
Shaver, Lloyd 1913,-1914,
    1916
Shaver, Lori 1915
Shaver, Mildred 1913-1916
Smith, Clarence 1918-1928
Smith, George 1920
Smith, Marion 1918-1923
Smith, Percy 1918-1926
Smith, Walter 1918-1928
Stewart, Hazel 1923
Sutton, Delvin 1926-1928
Sutton, Wesley 1926-1928
Taylor, Cora 1913
Tidwell, Ernest 1914-1915
Trask, Billie 1929